Gaudí and Modernism in Barcelona

H KLICZKOWSKI

Gaudí and Modernism in Barcelona

Publisher: Paco Asensio

Publishing coordinator: Cristina Montes

Photography: © Miquel Tres

Text: Raül Garcia i Aranzueque

Translation: Edward Krasny

Proofreading: Juliet King

Art direction: Mireia Casanovas Soley

Graphic desing: Emma Termes Parera

Layout: Soti Mas-Bagà

ISBN: 84-89439-87-7

D.L.: B-4739-02

Editorial project:

LOFT Publications

Domènec, 9 2-2

08012 Barcelona. Spain

Tel.: +34 93 218 30 99

Fax: +34 93 237 00 60

e-mail: loft@loftpublications.com

www.loftpublications.com

Printed in:

Anman Artes Gráficas. Sabadell. Barcelona. Spain

February 2002

1. Alcaldía de Hostafrancs

2. Casa Bellesguard

3. Casa Golferichs

4. Grill Room

5. Casa Arnús

6. Casa Roviralta

7. Casa de la Lactància

8. Casa Pérez Samanillo

9. Convento de Valldonzella

10. Fábrica Casarramona

11. Casa Company

12. Plaza de Toros Monumental

13. Caixa de Pensions

Satined Glass Windows

Furnishings

Continuation

p. 66 - 73

- Palau Güell
- Mercat de la Boqueria
- Els 4 Gats
- Palau de la Música
- Casa Calvet
- Casa Lleó Morera
- Casa Amatller
- Casa Batlló
- Palau Montaner
- Casa Milà, la Pedrera
- Casa Terrades
- Sagrada Família
- Hospital de Sant Pau
- Park Güell, Casa Museu Gaudí
- Casa Vicens
- Farolas de la plaza Reial
- Hotel España

- Hotel Peninsular
- Cafè de l'Òpera
- Casa Dr. Genové
- Antigua Casa Figueras
- Reial Acad. de Ciències i Arts
- Farmàcia Nadal
- Ateneu Barcelonès
- Casa Pascual i Pons
- Catalana de Gas
- Forn Sarret
- Casas Rocamora
- Editorial Montaner i Simon
- Casa Dolors Calm
- Casa Fargas
- Farmàcia Bolós
- Casa Juncosa
- Casa Josep i Ramon Queraltó

- Farolas de Esteve Falqués
- Casa Josefa Villanueva
- Casa Jaume Forn
- Conservatori Municipal de Música
- Casa Llopis i Bofill
- Casa Thomas
- Can Serra
- Casa Sayrach
- Casa Bonaventura Ferrer
- Casa Fuster
- Casa Comalat
- Palau del Baró de Quadras
- Casa Macaya
- Casa Planells
- Museu de Zoologia
- Museu d' Art Modern

Casa Arnús

For the knowledgeable reader already acquainted with Barcelona's main Modernist buildings, described in the first work of this collection, this book proposes a different way to discover the great number of Modernist treasures the city holds. The idea is to enjoy all the charms of the Catalan capital, lifting one's gaze to admire Modernism's artistic legacy in private residences, monuments, restaurants, businesses, churches, etc.

The identifying traits of Modernism are both unmistakeable and diffuse. Unmistakeable because no other artistic school possesses such a distinctive character, so distinctive; and diffuse because, as with any other movement, given each artist's cultural and historic influences, the different works do not lend themselves to easy classification. With that in mind, this book is intended as a fitting and effective tool. Our proposal includes straying outside Barcelona's Modernist heart, the city centre and Eixample area, to follow the Modernist trail through the city's other neighbourhoods, some of which were, in their day, independent towns. Four of the chapters deal with buildings in the uppermost reaches of the city, at the foot of Mont Tibidabo, where a fair number of the bourgeoisie of the

Barcelonans have begun to turn their attention away from the city centre and towards other areas to admire their valuable Modernist patrimony

Fábrica Casarramona

Casa Golferichs

period sought peace and quiet away from the growing hustle and bustle of the city centre. Since then, this part of the city has gradually become an area of upper-class residences, as well as a desirable location for many prestigious companies and foundations.

The Catalan capital, it is said, lived many years with its back to the sea, which it did not rediscover until dozens of kilometres of shoreline, literally closed off for decades, were restored for public use. Something similar has occurred with the mountains. Only in recent years has Barcelona turned its gaze towards the city's "green lung", and in doing so has begun to appreciate its estimable Modernist heritage. The Arnús and Bellesguard houses are striking examples of buildings that went almost unnoticed and that now form part of the city's iconography. In our journey beyond the confines of the Eixample we will stop off at Sants, an independent municipality that

Convento de Valldonzella

Alcaldía de Hostafrancs

was absorbed by Barcelona in 1897. There we find the Alcaldía de Hostafrancs, a building of unquestionable value yet utterly ignored by the usual tourist itineraries, and even by the Barcelonans themselves. This building houses stunning stained glass windows that are the pride of Sants residents.

We have included in this book two special chapters: one dedicated to stained glass and the other to furnishings. It is our humble tribute to the work of so many Modernist artists and artisans whose work has been somewhat overshadowed by the fame of the architects. If not for their contributions, this artistic movement would not have shone as brightly as

Stained glass window

Batlló bench

it did. The architects themselves placed great importance on these elements in the creation of their works, as evidenced by the fact that Gaudí often turned his genius to furniture design.

We also seek to show, once again, the true dimension of the Modernist movement, which transcended the merely artistic to become a style of life. Thus, beyond the numerous residences — in many cases symbols of ostentation — built for the most well-to-do families of the period, Modernist architecture was embraced by a great number of businesses: savings banks such as Caixa de Pensions; factories such as the Casarramona textile mill; and the Plaza de Toros Monumental, the world's only Modernist bullring.

We want to show the true dimension of the Modernist movement, which trascended artistic tendencies to become a style of life

With this book we seek to offer the reader new means to enjoy the innumerable subtleties concealed in each Modernist work of the grand capital of Modernism: Barcelona.

The auditorium hosts the district plenary sessions, and frequent civil marriages. The authorities have respected the battered old wooden dais and the carved wooden benches, as beautiful as they are uncomfortable.

Alcaldía de Hostafrancs

1895

Jaume Gustà i Bondia 1854-1936

Creu Coberta, 104

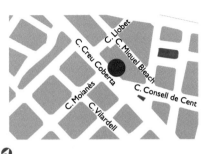

The name of this building – currently the offices of the Barcelona district of Sants-Montjuïc – is the source of certain confusion, since it would seem to indicate that the neighbourhood of Hostafrancs is a municipality, which it has never been. The area presently occupied by Hostafrancs was ceded in 1839 by the town of Santa Maria de Sants to the city of Barcelona, and in 1864 the city government of the Catalan capital located the deputy mayor's office on the plot now occupied by the Sants-Montjuïc district offices. The inhabitants of the neighbourhood shortened the official name Tinença d'Alcaldia to Alcaldia (mayor's office), and so it has been called through the years.

Although in the Modernist style, the building contains unmistakable Noucentista elements and symbols typical of the period in which it was built. Its Modernist character can be seen in the extremely detailed ornamentation and the abundance of floral elements.

The façade contains such interesting details as the ironwork from which the bells are suspended, the stone relief work, the balcony and window. But the building's real treasure is found inside: the auditorium. Going up the stairs to this room, one will notice the delicate work of the handrail, and, in the first-floor vestibule, the skylight with its spectacular stained glass. The twelve wrought iron seahorses supporting the skylight are also noteworthy.

The stunningly beautiful stained glass windows of the auditorium are a fine example of Noucentista artwork. Painter Francesc Labarta shunned the lyrical excesses of Modernism and imbued the windows with Mediterranean classicism and prevalence of form over the colours associated with that artistic style.

The stained glass combines mythological characters with scenes from the day-to-day life of the period, especially people at work.

From the outside, the building looks like a castle. Built of stone and brick, its looming profile dominates the setting. The slender tower is crowned by a four-pointed cross, a typically Gaudiesque feature.

Casa Bellesguard

1900-1909

Antoni Gaudí 1852-1926

Bellesguard, 16-20

The name of this building describes its most notable feature. From high on the Collserola mountain, Casa Bellesguard – Bellavista in Spanish – offers commanding views over Barcelona.

The building is also known for its former owner, Jaume Figueras, as Casa Figueras. Gaudí built it over the scant ruins of the summer residence of the last Catalan king, Martin the Humane (d. 1410). Such historic circumstances inspired the architect, who created a work of neo-Gothic character reminiscent of medieval castles. On the exterior Gaudí pays personal homage to medieval Catalan splendour, while the interior reflects his typically Modernist flights of fancy.

Those fortunate enough to see the inside of this private estate will appreciate the magnitude of the contrast between the austerity of the exterior and the exuberance of the interior, where lively colours and rounded forms predominate. Worthy of special attention are such ornamental details as the mosaics designed by Domènech Sugranyes and the splendid combination with the wrought iron elements.

After the visit, it is highly recommendable to have a good look at the metropolis below and – why not? – try to identify the city's most emblematic monuments and buildings.

Casa Golferichs 1901

Joan Rubió i Bellver 1871-1952

Gran Via de les Corts Catalanes, 491

W ith gratitude to the neighbourhood movement whose actions made it possible for us to celebrate today the centennial of this building, restored for the use of its citizens. Casa Golferichs 1901-2001." That inscription, on a plaque on the main façade of the building, sums up the happy ending of a Modernist work which, like so many others in the city, was rescued from property speculators by public pressure.

Casa Golferichs was commissioned to the architect Joan Rubió, who worked closely with Gaudí, by Macari Golferichs, a wealthy merchant and lover of art and culture whose greatest wish was to live in a Modernist home that would stand out among the uniform dwellings of the Eixample. To realise that dream, Rubió projected a single-family home in which he reserved part of the plot for a small garden, thus breaking with the monotonous layout of the blocks of the Eixample.

The Golferichs family lived in the house until the summer of 1936. At the outbreak of the Civil War, it was confiscated by a group of libertarian militants with the aim of turning it into a people's university. After the war, the house and an adjoining building were ceded to the order of the Dominicans of the Presentation, who founded a religious school.

In this work, the architect established his architectural style by updating Gothic forms and using local materials such as brick and carved stone. The influence of his work with Gaudí can be seen in some parts of the interior.

At present, Casa Golferichs houses the Fundació Carles Pi i Sunyer, a number of services of the Eixample district, including a children's play centre and the Fundació Català-Roca, a photography school.

Grill Room 1902

Ricard de Campmany

Escudellers, 8

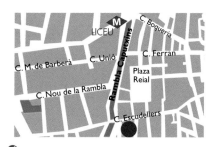

Carrer Escudellers, running through the heart of Barcelona's old quarter, is an example of cultural diversity. The street features everything from establishments decorated in vanguard style to typical neighbourhood bars with their habitual clientele, eyes glued to the football match on TV. The Grill Room is the requisite touch of Modernism on a Barcelona street that prides itself on being cosmopolitan.

This restaurant, where it is not easy to find a free table, was decorated by Ricard de Campmany, who adopted a characteristically Modernist aesthetic, immediately perceptible in the façade. It is completely finished in wood, and an enormous sign spells out the name of the establishment in typical lettering of the time. The interior as well preserves the signs of identity of this artistic movement, with a great profusion of curved lines and floral motifs in carved wood and ornamental ironwork. The bar stands out for its great size, and particularly interesting are the small decorative details scattered throughout the premises.

The Grill Room is a good place to start an urban expedition in search of more Modernist establishments in Barcelona's historic centre that reflect the artistic whims of a good part of the petty bourgeoisie of the period.

The Grill Room's main façade stands out among the other, far more recent establishments along carrer Escudellers. The particular character of these premises is a major draw for the restaurant's customers.

Inside the establishment, one can appreciate some of the identifying traits of Modernism, such as the profusion of curved lines and delicate floral motifs.

Due to its rather generous proportions, the bar is a prominent piece of the interior decoration.

Casa Arnús 1903

Enric Sagnier 1858-1931

Manuel Arnús, 1-31

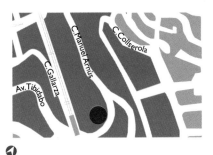

The name by which this private home is known is written on the main gate to the estate: El Pinar. Abounding in pines, the estate is a lush, vevitable forest which also includes numerous palm trees and various other species. Out of the midst of such exuberant vegetation rises this neo-Gothic palace, set on the lower slope of Mont Tibidabo, just above the cable car station up to the amusement park.

Over the years, the building has become an icon of this part of the city, mainly for its phantasmagoric appearance when lit up at night. Nearby, a fair number of bars attract hundreds of young and not-so-young folk who enjoy the nightlife while the city slumbers below.

Casa Arnús is a single-family residence laid out in the shape of a cross with two towers, one octagonal and the other square, on the west façade. The well-conceived combination of gabled roofs covered in ceramic tiling of varied colours, masonry, stuccoed stretches of wall and sgraffiti, all masterfully laid out, affords the overall structure its extraordinary beauty.

Inside, the dining room furnishings, the work of the Modernist cabinet-maker Joan Busquets, with plentiful floral motifs, are outstanding. The round window of this room offers a splendid view of Barcelona.

Enric Sagnier built a large number of homes for the refined bourgeoisie of the period. Sagnier left his special neo-Gothic stamp on CasaArnús, and many other works.

By night, the lighting emphasises the house's phantasmagoric appearance. The way the building stands alone, set in the middle of a thick pine forest, contributes to its special ambience.

Two columns indicate the access to the porch of the main entrance, which features arches with curved, elegant lines.

FRARE—BLANCH

PARKING
El Asador de Aranda
Teodoro Roviralta, 14

Casa Roviralta 1903-1913

Joan Rubió i Bellver 1871-1952

Avenida Tibidabo, 31

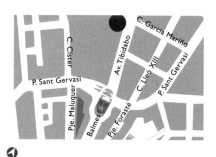

C asa Roviralta should be visited at night, when lit. That is when the building appears like something out of a fairytale. In the flood lamps the white of the stuccoed walls shines immaculate in contrast to the brown of the eaves and brick. The capricious forms of the roof, doors and windows put the final touches on its dream-like appearance.

Joan Rubió built this house over the ruins of a farmhouse called El Frare Blanc (The White Friar) beacuse it once belonged to an old Dominican convent, and that is how it is popularly known today.

The building was designed as a single-family home in a residential area of Barcelona where, at the beginning of the century, a large number of houses were built following the garden-city model, in a departure from the uniformity of the dwellings of the Eixample. Casa Roviralta one of the last of Rubió's truly Modernist works, which shows off his trademarks despite details that recall the style of Puig i Cadafalch.

The building now houses a restaurant, El Asador de Aranda, specialising in Castilian cuisine. Visitors can admire the interior of the premises while enjoying the house specialities.

Although there were some changes made in the interior when it was converted into a restaurant, the original basic structure remains as it was. The superb sundial on the façade is worth the look.

The interior decoration of the house, more austere than other Modernist buildings, abounds in white mosaics that highlight the structure. Especially interesting are the rooms converted for dining, as well as the kitchen with its beautiful brickwork vault.

The skylight gives the building a glow that brings out the interior mosaics and stained glass. Many Modernist architects gave this feature great importance in the conception of their works: the effect of natural light was a defining factor in their design.

Casa de la Lactància

1908-1913

P. Falqués 1850-1916 **y A. de Falguera** 1876-1945

Gran Via de les Corts Catalanes, 475-477

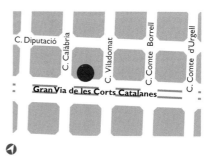

The history of this building in the Gran Via of Barcelona, is curious. As fate would have it, the structure has provided shelter for people in both the first and last moments of life. What was originally a maternity hospital now houses an old people's home, where the elderly chat, receive visits from their families and play dominos.

The stone pediment on the main façade contains a set of sculptured figures by Eusebi Arnau which tells of the buildings' original use: the central figure, who represents the city, is a woman breastfeeding a child. She is surrounded by a group of women who put infants in her arms for care. The scene is crowned by the Barcelona coat of arms and the words "Lactancia Municipal" in lettering that recalls that of the Monumental bullring, also in Gran Via.

The building was projected as a small palace between Gothic-inspired dividing walls, like many of the buildings of the period. In the interior patio, a skylight illuminates the colourful mosaics on the walls and floors, predominated by pastels, especially green. Also outstanding in the patio are the ceramic skirting and the frieze.

The rooms on the upper floor open onto a perimeter balcony with wrought iron corbels, from where one has a better view of the stained glass skylight.

The building was enlarged and restored in 1968, and the renovation that respected its Modernist features.

Casa Pérez Samanillo 1909-1910

Joan J. Hervás 1851-1912

Balmes, 169 / Avenida Diagonal, 502-504

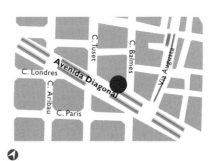

After amassing a large fortune in the Philippines, Luis Pérez Samanillo returned to Barcelona ready to show off his new economic status. Like many other members of the bourgeoisie, chose the upper Eixample to build his home. His residence was an authentic Modernist mansion, the façade of which includes a noteworthy large oval window, known in Catalan architectural slang as a "peixera" (fishbowl).

Since 1948 the building has belonged to the Círculo Ecuestre defined by the president as a social club for entrepreneurs, in the style of British clubs. Although it started out as club for horsemen – and thus the name – through the years it has come to be one of the must exclusive clubs of Barcelona high society. The luxurious premises of the Ecuestre host all sorts of business events: presentations, business dinners, meetings, etc., but also gatherings of friends who meet at the club to sip fine cognac and leaf through the international financial press comfortably seated in elegant armchairs.

The interior decor tends toward sybaritism, both in the sumptuous furnishings and the elegance of the walls, floors and ceilings, all perfectly conserved. The vestibule offers examples of the fine work of the artisans of the period: in the wooden floor, figures of dragons, harps and floral motifs; a mosaic floor; and the curvilinear door frames.

In 1910 the Barcelona city government awarded Casa Pérez Samanillo with the prize for best building. Its ostentatious appearance caused a great sensation at the time.

The interior decoration is a compendium of luxury and opulence. The Círculo Ecuestre is one of the most exclusive clubs in Barcelona.

Convento de Valldonzella 1910-1919

Bernardí Martorell Puig 1870-1937

Císter, 41-45

In the aftermath of the violent popular revolt that led to the Tragic Week of 1909, when hundreds of lives were lost and numerous churches destroyed, the nuns of the convent of Valldonzella found the peace they required for their monastic existence. The premises formerly housed he municipality of Sant Gervasi de Cassoles.

Thanks to its location at the foot of the Collserola ridge – Barcelona's "green lung" – behind the enormous walls of this fortress-like convent the nuns' peace and quiet seems assured even today. The area of Sant Gervasi, where it is located, is a reguge of tranquillity in the bustling Catalan capital. An upper-class neighbourhood dotted with prestigious foundations, renowned clinics and schools with students in uniform, unbreachable walls like those of the convent of Valldonzella it is the setting of many.

The most outstanding features of this exposed brick building are the temple with Latin cross, the outer door and the great cantenary arches inside, reminiscent of Gaudí. Worth a look is the cloister with its elegant arcs and exposed brick columns.

The Covent of Valldonzella is an oasis of peace, where the nuns find the tranquillity they need for their monastic life. The nuns also have large spaces in which to carry out their activities.

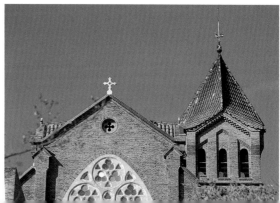

The most outstanding features of the cloister are the slender arcs and columns, built out of expposed brick.

Fábrica Casarramona

1911

Josep Puig i Cadafalch 1867-1956

Mèxic, 36-44

Fàbrica Casarramona, originally a spinning and weaving mill, demonstrates how Modernist art impregnated all spheres of Barcelona and Catalan society. Like this one, many Catalan factories, especially in the textile sector, were built by great architects of Catalan Modernism. Catalonia abounds in old textile colonies with buildings of notable artistic interest, which are even included today on tourist itineraries.

The Casarramona mill is a fine example of Modernist industrial architecture. With austere decoration, Puig i Cadafalch made the most out of the expressive qualities of brick, successfully combining the Medieval beauty of the building with its requisite industrial functionality. The neo-Gothic-style structure is striking, particularly the exposed brick façade, executed skilfully in grey iron with a succession of vertical lines over a horizontal plane.

From the towers that once held water pressure control tanks, one has a splendid view of the nearby Palau Nacional de Montjuïc. The complex occupies a full square block on the edge of the Eixample at the foot of Montjuïc, an area that was well outside the city centre when the mill was built. The building now belongs to the Fundació Caixa d'Estalvis i Pensions de Barcelona, and is a centre for culture and the arts.

Modernist architects knew how to harmonise the artistic beauty of their works with the most prosaic needs, as seen in the numerous textile mills and colonies from this period that dot the Catalan landscape.

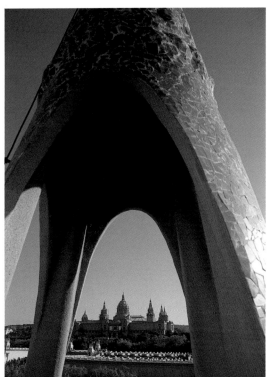

Casa Company 1911

Josep Puig i Cadafalch 1867-1956

Casanova, 203

odernist or Noucentista? The experts remain divided over which artistic movement this single-family residence in the Eixample belongs to. But all agree that the building belongs to Puig i Cadafalch's white period. The prestigious art historian Cirici Pellicer divided the Catalan architect's work into three periods: pink (which coincides with Modernism), white and yellow. The white period is marked by strong influence of Viennese Secessionism, which lends a very different style to this master's work.

In 1909, two years before he built Casa Company, Puig i Cadafalch travelled to Germany where he soaked up the local architecture and town planning, as evidenced in the numerous laudatory articles he wrote upon his return to Catalonia. His admiration soon translated into numerous influences on his architectural style.

Careful contemplation of Casa Company allows one to appreciate the Alpine touches in the building, comparable to with the style of many houses in Tyrol, Switzerland, southern Germany and the Italian Alps. A good example are the sgraffiti on the façade, terminating in undulating eaves, as on many houses of the Alpine areas. The two chimneys sheathed in mosaic are examples of the architect's Modernist sensibility.

Since 1982 the building has housed the Museu i Centre d'Estudis de l'Esport Doctor Melcior Colet (named for the gynaecologist who donated the building for the museum). It now contains a permanent collection dedicated to sports, as well as temporary exhibitions.

Santiago Marco Urrutia refurbished the interior of the house in 1940, after it was acquired by Dr Melcior Colet.

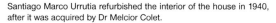

Through various reformations, the house has acquired an eclectic style, including Central Euroean architectural influences and Arabic elements.

The white and blue tiles, the elegant lettering and forms on the exterior reveal the Modernist character of a work that was built in the latter period of this artistic movement.

Plaza de Toros Monumental 1916

I. Mas Morell 1881-1953 / D. Sugrañes Gras 1878-1938

Gran Via de les Corts Catalanes, 749

The Monumental Bullring offers the tourist a number of attractions. Those who like clichés will enjoy the chance to witness a typical Spanish bullfight, even at the risk of certain disappointment due to the meagre presence of locals in the stands, in contrast with the abundance of foreigners; and for architecture aficionados, the sight of the only Modernist bullring in the world, built in the last years of this artistic movement.

What is striking about the Monumental are the Arabesque touches, the white and blue tiling on the exterior and the egg-shaped domes on the towers. The architects Ignasi Mas and Domènec Sugrañes executed their work on the bullring, actually built two years previously. They completely refurbished the building, and enlarged its significantly.

The result is a harmonious combination of forms, highlighted by the exterior ceramic tiling over a base of exposed brick. The contrasting materials and colours give the work a great ornamental richness, including the elegant typography chosen for the lettering, which maintains the use of tiles and characteristic chromatic play of whites and blues.

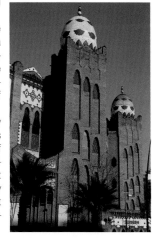

From carrer Marina one can see the Sagrada Família, and, looking seaward, an example of the city's contemporary architecture: the twin towers of the Port Olímpic.

To remain economically viable, the Monumental is now used for all sorts of events. In addition to bullfights, the premises host concerts and, on many occasions, this Modernist work holds an immense circus tent.

The façades of the building clearly show its Noucentista influence. By the time the Caixa de Pensions was built the new architectural trend was beginning to overtake Modernism and would slowly replace it in the building in the city.

Caixa de Pensions 1917

Enric Sagnier 1858-1931

Via Laietana, 56-58

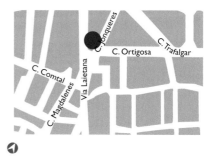

The former main office of the Caixa de Pensions is a further example of Modernist architects' obsession with reviving Catalan Gothic, albeit adapted to the tastes of the period. For this building in Via Laietana, Enric Sagnier projected a neo-Medieval work with ecclesiastical touches – two features that are patent in the steeple-like tower and the materials of the façade: rough textured ashlars and smoothly carved stone. The architect did not concern himself with adorning the building with elements that would easily identify it as a savings bank. The only reference to the building's use is found in a set of sculptured figures by Manuel Fuxà called "L'estalvi" (The saving), which can be seen on one corner of the façade. A woman dressed in a tunic holds a chest, representing a money box, while an old man with a cane rests his head on her, and a woman and daughter seem to plead for her shelter. Beside the sculpture is the original name of the savings institution: "Caja de Pensiones para la Vejez y de Ahorros", a synthesis of the sculptured scene.

While this building was under construction, Enric Sagnier built another in carrer Jonqueres, just off Via Laietana, for the same institution. This building features another interesting group sculpture by Eusebi Arnau.

Stained glass windows

odernist stained glass clearly demonstrates the importance of the inspiration its artists found in Gothic works. In Barcelona, Modernism's most emblematic city, there exist many examples of the close relationship between the two artistic currents. And there is no better way to appreciate the intensive use of stained glass ornamentation than a tour of the Barri Gòtic and the Eixample. Still, the works of each artist and of each movement show their distinctive marks. It is precisely this great range of personal styles that makes it often so difficult to fit some stained-glass windows neatly into one or the other artistic school. Further, as tends to happen, two movements of the magnitude of Modernism and Noucentisme overlapped in time, and even mixed. Thus, in buildings considered Modernist, such as the Alcaldía de Hostafrancs, described in this book, one can see stunning Noucentista stained glass windows, which are the building's greatest treasure.

Modernist stained glass is characterised by the preponderance of colour, which plays with the brightness and glow that it confers on light. The Noucentistes, on the other hand, emphasised form and lines, and light was not afforded the same importance. The result is less luminosity, less transparency. The windows also bear witness to the cultural references of each movement. The Modernist fascination with the Nordic cultures and the Noucentista exaltation of Mediterranean classicism are embodied in these striking and seductive works of art.

1. Casa Pérez Samanillo
2. Conservatori Municipal de Música
3. Alcaldía de Hostafrancs
4, 12. Casa Ametller
5. Casa Roviralta
6,7, 8, 11. Alcaldía de Hostafrancs
9. Palacio del Barón de Quadras
10, 13. Casa Arnús
14. Convento de Valldonzella

Furnishings

The extraordinary fame that Modernism has gained thanks to its architectural works should not overshadow the brilliant work that its artists did inside the buildings, and which were decisive in solidifying the character of this multidisciplinary, artistic and cultural movement. Modernist furnishings are a very important part of this estimable artistic legacy. This is demonstrated by the fact that Gaudí himself designed a great number of furnishings for his own buildings and those of other architects.

Modernist artisans excelled at the art of carving and shaping wood, transforming the noble material into true works of art. A taste for curved lines and profusion of details, also characteristic of the architecture, was their inspiration. Thus, the Modernist movement brought back the ancient art of sculpting wood, and at the same time combined wood with other basic materials such as wrought iron and ceramic tiling.

With Modernism in Barcelona and Catalonia having regained its prestige in recent years , the value of the original furniture of the period has likewise risen extraordinarily. Many homes, Modernist or not, preserve all sorts of treasured tables, chairs, sideboards and other furnishings, comprising a noble testimony to the artistic ambitions and tastes of a period of exceptional creativity in the 20th century.

Furnishings designed by Gaudí

1. Batlló bench
2. Calvet bench
3, 7, 8, 9, 11. Casa Milà Interiors
4. Calvet armchair
5. Calvet stool
6. Batlló chair
10. Calvet mirror

The Modernist Route. Continuation

14. Palau Güell 1886

Nou de la Rambla, 3-5

15. Mercat de la Boqueria 1874

La Rambla, 91

16. Els 4 Gats 1894

Montsió, 3

17. Palau de la Música Catalana 1905

Sant Pere més Alt, 13

18. Casa Calvet 1900

Casp, 48

19. Casa Lleó Morera 1902

Paseo de Gràcia, 35

20. Casa Amatller 1898
Paseo de Gràcia, 41

21. Casa Batlló 1905
Paseo de Gràcia, 43

22. Palau Montaner 1889
Mallorca, 278

23. Casa Milà, la Pedrera 1906
Paseo de Gràcia, 92

26. Hospital de Sant Pau 1905
Sant Antoni Maria Claret, 167

24. Casa Terrades 1903
Diagonal, 416

25. Sagrada Família 1881
Plaza de la Sagrada Família

27. Park Güell 1900
Olot, s/n

28. Casa Vicens 1883

Carolines, 18-24

29. Farolas de la plaza Reial 1878

Plaza Reial

30. Hotel España 1903

Sant Pau, 9-11

31. Hotel Peninsular

Sant Pau, 34

32. Cafè de l'Òpera 1929

La Rambla, 74

33. Casa Dr. Genové

La Rambla, 77

34. Antigua Casa Figueres 1902
La Rambla, 83

35. R. Acadèmia de Ciències i Arts 1883
La Rambla, 115

36. Farmàcia Nadal 1850
La Rambla, 121

40. Forn Sarret
Girona, 73

37. Ateneu Barcelonès 1836
Canuda, 6

38. Casa Pascual i Pons 1891
Paseo de Gràcia, 2-4

39. Catalana de Gas 1895
Portal de l'Àngel, 20-22

41. Casas Rocamora 1917

Paseo de Gràcia, 6-14

42. Editorial Montaner i Simon 1880

Aragó, 255

43. Casa Dolors Calm 1902

Rambla Catalunya, 54

44. Casa Fargas

Rambla Catalunya, 47

45. Farmàcia Bolós 1902

Rambla Catalunya, 77

46. Casa Juncosa 1907

Rambla Catalunya, 76-78

47. C. Josep i Ramon Queraltó 1907

Rambla Catalunya, 88

48. Farolas de Esteve Falqués 1906

Paseo de Gràcia

49. Casa Josefa Villanueva 1909

València, 312

50. Casa Jaume Forn 1904

València, 285

51. Conservatori M. de Música 1916

Bruc, 112

52. Casa Llopis Bofill

Bailèn, 113

53. Casa Thomas 1898

Mallorca, 293

54. Can Serra 1908

Rambla Catalunya, 126

55. Casa Sayrach 1918

Diagonal, 423

56. Casa Bonaventura Ferrer 1906

Paseo de Gràcia, 113

57. Casa Fuster

Paseo de Gràcia, 132

58. Casa Comalat 1911

Diagonal, 442

59. Palau del Baró de Quadras 1904

Diagonal, 373

60. Casa Macaya 1901

Paseo Sant Joan, 108

61. Casa Planells 1924

Diagonal, 332

62. Museu de Zoologia 1888

Parque de la Ciutadella

63. Museu d'Art Modern

Parque de la Ciutadella

Photographs © Pere Planells:
14, 18, 21, 23, 25, 27, 28

Photographs © Melba Levick:
16, 17, 19, 20, 22, 24, 26

1. Alcaldía de Hostafrancs
2. Casa Bellesguard
   (Out of map)
3. Casa Golferichs
4. Grill Room
5. Casa Arnús (El Pinar)
   (Out of map)
6. Casa Roviralta
   (Out of map)
7. Casa de la Lactància
8. Casa Pérez Samanillo
9. Convento de Valldonzella
   (Out of map)
10. Fábrica Casarramona
11. Casa Company
12. Plaza de Toros
    Monumental
13. Caixa de Pensions
14. Palau Güell
15. Mercat de la Boqueria
16. Els 4 Gats
17. Palau de la Música
18. Casa Calvet
19. Casa Lleó Morera
20. Casa Amatller. Punto de
    información modernista
21. Casa Batlló
22. Palau Montaner
23. Casa Milà, la Pedrera
24. Casa Terrades, Casa
    de les Punxes
25. Sagrada Família
26. Hospital de la Santa
    Creu i Sant Pau
27. Park Güell, Casa Museu
    Gaudí
28. Casa Vicens
29. Farolas de la plaza Reial
30. Hotel España
31. Hotel Peninsular

32. Cafè de l'Òpera
33. Casa Dr. Genové
34. Antigua Casa Figueres
35. Reial Acadèmia de
    Ciències i Arts
36. Farmàcia Nadal
37. Ateneu Barcelonès
38. Casa Pascual i Pons
39. Catalana de Gas
40. Forn Sarret
41. Casas Rocamora
42. Editorial Montaner
    i Simon
43. Casa Dolors Calm
44. Casa Fargas
45. Farmàcia Bolós
46. Casa Juncosa
47. Casa Josep i Ramon
    Queraltó
48. Farolas de Esteve
    Falqués
49. Casa Josefa Villanueva
50. Casa Jaume Forn
51. Conservatori Municipal
    de Música
52. Casa Llopis Bofill
53. Casa Thomas
54. Can Serra
55. Casa Sayrach
56. Casa Bonaventura
    Ferrer
57. Casa Fuster
58. Casa Comalat
59. Palau del Baró
    de Quadras
60. Casa Macaya
61. Casa Planells
62. Museu de Zoologia
63. Museu d'Art Modern

Practical Information

ℹ Centre del Modernisme

Paseo de Gràcia, 41 (Casa Amatller)

Tel.: 934 880 139

www.rutamodernisme.com

Horario: laborables de 10 a 19 h y domingos y festivos de 10 a 14 h.

El centro facilita un multipase que da derecho a un descuento del 50% en las entradas de todos los monumentos de la ruta y tiene una validez de un mes. Además, ofrece una explicación sobre las fachadas de la "manzana de la discordia" –Casa Batlló, Casa Amatller y Casa Lleó Morera– seis veces al día en español y en inglés.

Otras webs donde puede encontrarse información sobre el Modernismo:

www.gaudiclub.com

www.barcelona-on-line.es

www.horitzo.es/expo2000.

Visits

The visits to buidings listed below all start out from the same point, Plaça Catalunya.

1. Alcaldía de Hostafrancs

Creu Coberta, 104-106

Metro HOSTAFRANCS (line 1)

Take line 1 to HOSTAFRANCS. Once at the station, take the Moianès exit that meets the street Creu Coberta, where the building is located.

2. Casa Bellesguard

Bellesguard, 16-20

Metro PENITENTS (line 3) and Bus line 60

Take metro line 3. Outside the Penitents station, catch the bus line 60 and get out at the stop Ronda de Dalt-Bellesguard. The building is located at the beginning of the street.

3. Casa Golferichs

Gran Vía de les Corts Catalanes, 491

Metro URGELL (line 1)

Take metro line 1 from Catalunya. Once outside the URGELL station, head towards Gran Via. The building is past the street Comte Borrell.

4. Grill Room

Escudellers, 8 - Pasaje. Escudellers, 2

Metro LICEU (line 3)

Walk down the Rambla to the plaza Teatre. Once there, go down the first street and at the first corner, turn right.

5. Casa Arnús

Manuel Arnús, 1-31 - plaza del Funicular, s/n

Metro VALL D' HEBRON (línea 3)

Train Ferrocarriles FGC AVDA TIBIDABO (line U7).
The Tibidabo station exits at Avenida Tibidabo. There, take the Tramvia Blau (Blue Tram) and get out at the last stop. The building is located behind the plaza Doctor Andreu.

6. Casa Roviralta

Avda Tibidabo, 31

Train Ferrocarriles FGC AVDA TIBIDABO (line U7).
The Tibidabo train station exit is located directly in front of Avenida Tibidabo.

.7. Casa de la Lactància

Gran Via de les Corts Catalanes, 475-477

Metro ROCAFORT (line 1)

Take the exit Gran Via/Calàbria. Once outside, walk down Gran Vía. The building is located in the first block.

8. Casa Pérez Samanillo

Balmes, 169-169 bis - Avda Diagonal, 502-504

Bus PG. GRÀCIA- CASP (line 17)

Take the bus to the stop Via Augusta- Séneca. Walk down to Diagonal until it intersects with Balmes. Walk up Balmes. The building is located in the first block.

9. Convento de Valldonzella

Císter, 41-45

Bus (line 58)

Take bus line 58 from plaza Catalunya. Get out at Passeig Sant Gervasi-Folgueroles. Walk down the street Císter for two blocks to reach the building.

10. Fábrica Casarramona

Mèxic, 36-44

Metro ESPANYA (line 1)

Take metro line 1 to Espanya. Once outside, walk down Gran Vía until it intersects with the street Mèxic. Walk to the end of this street.

11. Casa Company

Casanova, 203

Metro DIAGONAL (line 3 and 5)

Take metro line 3. Once outside the Diagonal station, walk up to Diagonal and catch bus line 6. Get out at Diagonal-Francesc Macià. Walk back down Diagonal until it intersects with Casanova. Walk down Casanova and go down a side street.

12. Plaza de Toros Monumental

Gran Vía de les Corts Catalanes, 749

Metro MONUMENTAL (line 2), MARINA (line 1)

Take metro line 2. The building is located directly in front of the Monumental station exit.

13. Caixa de Pensions

Via Laietana, 56-58

Metro CATALUNYA (line 1)

Take the road Ronda Sant Pere to Plaza Urquinaona. Walk down the left side of Via Laietana. The building is located at the first corner.

Other titles by the publishing company

Fundición, 15 Polígono Industrial Santa Ana 28529 Rivas-Vaciamadrid Madrid Tel. 34 91 666 50 01 Fax 34 91 301 26 83 asppan@asppan.com www.onlybook.com

78

The Best of Lofts
ISBN (E/GB): 95-09575-84-4

The Best of Bars & Restaurants
ISBN (E/GB): 95-09575-86-0

The Best of American Houses
ISBN (E/GB): 98-79778-17-0

Interiores minimalistas/Minimalist Interiors
ISBN (E/GB): 98-79778-16-2

Lofts minimalistas/Minimalist lofts
ISBN (E/GB): 84-89439-55-9

Estancias Argentinas
ISBN (E/GB): 987-97781-9-7

Guggenheim
ISBN (E): 84-89439-52-4
ISBN (GB): 84-89439-53-2
ISBN (D): 84-89439-54-0
ISBN (P): 84-89439-63-X

Hotels. Designer & Design
Hoteles. Arquitectura y Diseño
ISBN (E/GB): 84-89439-61-3

Cafés. Designer & Design
Cafés. Arquitectura y Diseño
ISBN (E/GB): 84-89439-69-9

E: Spanish text   GB: English text   IT: Italian text   D: German text   P: portuguese text   J: Japanese text

Pubs
ISBN: (E) 84-89439-68-0

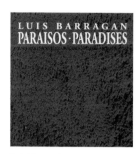

Luis Barragán
ISBN: (E/GB) 987-9474-02-3

Andrea Mantegna
ISBN: (E) 987-9474-10-4

Claude Monet
ISBN: (E) 987-9474-03-1

Rembrandt
ISBN: (E) 987-9474-09-0

Francisco Goya
ISBN: (E) 987-9474-11-2

Álvaro Siza
ISBN: (E) 84-89439-70-2
ISBN: (P) 972-576-220-7

Autos de Cuba
ISBN: (E) 84-89439-62-1

Veleros de época
ISBN (E): 987-9474-06-6

80

Los encantos de Barcelona/
Barcelona Style
ISBN (E): 84-89439-56-7
ISBN (GB): 84-89439-57-5

Barcelona de noche/
Barcelona by night
ISBN: (E)   84-89439-71-0
ISBN: (GB) 84-89439-72-9

Gaudí. Obra completa/
Gaudí. The complete work

Bauhaus
ISBN (E): 98-79778-14-6

Antoni Gaudí
ISBN (E): 98-75130-09-5

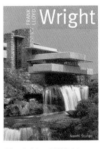

Frank Lloyd Wright
ISBN (E): 98-79778-11-1

Le Corbusier
ISBN (E): 98-79778-13-8

Frank Gehry
ISBN (E):   85868-879-5
ISBN (GB): 1-85868-879-5

La vida y obras de Antoni Gaudí
ISBN (E): 950-9575-78-X